BOUND BY THE
DEBT DEMON

It's time to stop living in the red

Donald G. Payne

Unless otherwise indicated, all Scripture quotations are taken from the *King James Version* of the Bible.

Published by: Garret Enterprises LLC

ISBN- 978-1-60458-374-8
Second Edition

Bound by the debt demon. Copyright ©2008, by Donald G. Payne. All rights reserved. Printed in the United States of America. For more information contact Garret Enterprises, LLC, Southfield, MI, 48076.

      Email address: dgp@mrdonaldpayne.com

      Web Address: www.mrdonaldpayne.com

Disclaimer: This publication is intended solely for the enjoyment of the reader concerning the pitfalls of being financially over-extended. The views contained within this booklet are the opinions of the writer and they should not be misconstrued as a professional opinion or professional advice. This book may also be considered as fiction.

This book is dedicated to

Roosevelt Payne Sr., whose wisdom and knowledge helped me to become a better man.

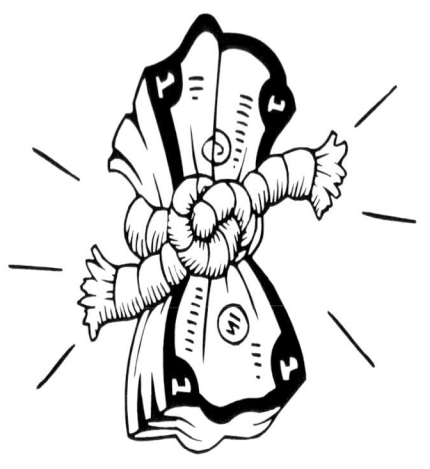

"Watch out! Be on your guard against all kinds of greed; a man's life does not consist in the abundance of his possessions."

-Luke 12:15

Table of Contents

Introduction 1
Ask Yourself 3
The Way I See It 7
Joy No More 15
You Are Not Alone 21
Misery Loves Company 25
More Bad News 31
Important Facts and Statistics 37
Sub-Primed 47
Help Is Here 51
The New Beginning 57
Sources 63

Foreword

I have known Donald Payne for several years and I admire his writing and his ongoing service to his community in so many endeavors.

This latest offering on handling and solving debt problems is not only helpful to individuals with problems, but also valuable information for people hoping to avoid future disaster. Donald Payne has had a long history of helping others; thus, he brings to debt counseling added assets gleaned from his experience in behavioral and habit disorders and dysfunction.

Donald takes a practical approach to solving debt problems both solvable and affordable without gimmicks or taking advantage. His methods work because he sincerely wishes to help others in one more way. People have profited from listening to and reading Donald's advice in the past.

Therefore, I can predict that this book will be valuable, affordable and easy to follow. Listen and take Donald's advice. It is wisely and expertly given with the utmost sincerity of his being.

Dale E. Cottrill, Ph.D.

Professor Emeritus of Speech Communication Arts, Humanities, Theater, English and Writing Disciplines

Macomb Community College - Michigan

Professor, Baker College of Michigan, Corporate Services Division

Other great works from Donald G. Payne
Living in the Red (volume 1)
Fear, Folly & Purpose
They're Just People

Coming Soon:
Do You Hear What I Hear?

PREFACE

This is a subject that has been on my mind for quite some time. I pray that my words will help you identify the problems with debt and how it affects your life. I would love to see the day when we all can live a stress-free life, oblivious to the debt demon.

I hate debt; I have a very strong aversion towards it. I hate the fact that debt is so easy to obtain and can consume you before you realize that you are in trouble; I know of so many people that have struggled with debt. I have even had my own struggles, some of which I have shared in this book.

With great sadness I have watched, being unable to help, as many of my loved ones have had to face foreclosures, repossessions, even bankruptcy. I am now seeing families that are splitting up after spending many years together; losing just about everything they have accumulated over the years.

After witnessing this downward spiral that many of my loved ones were facing, I began to write this book hoping that it would help someone understand that debt is just a privilege, a tool to help you in this earthly walk and should never bring you to a point that it burdens you. I have attempted to stress the importance of knowing your financial limitations by educating yourself using Biblical as well as practical knowledge that is available.

This knowledge has been obtained from various teachers in the world of finance, as well as Biblical scholars who have dedicated themselves to helping bring financial restoration to God's children. I believe that I have done my due diligence in research, and have taken the time to give you some of my extreme life lessons that in times past have helped others. It is my sincere goal that you overcome one of life's worst enemies, the debt demon.

With the numerous help books available, counseling institutions and the knowledge received from God's inspired Word (2 Timothy 3:16), anyone who wants to be free from the pressure and problems that debt can bring… SHALL: "meaning something will happen in the future, or is intended to happen" (Oxford University Press 2007)

Introduction

Debt has become common as a cold these days. If you have a job or some type of income, you qualify. Banking institutions and loan offices have made getting loans almost too easy, giving out sub-prime, adjustable rate loans and even interest-only loans. At one time they were accepting lower than normal credit scores, even letters of forgiveness to those who had blemishes on their credit reports. This situation has become a major problem for many, so bad that in 2007 the federal government had to create a special program to help those who were in financial ruin because of those loose lending conditions. (More on this later)

Debt has been destroying lives with the undo stress it causes. Americans have gotten to the point were they take pills to pay bills. People overwhelm themselves with credit worthiness, in what they believe to be some type of social being; they con themselves into thinking that they deserve to have something, or that they should be living the good life, just because they work everyday. This trap affects some people more than others; for the unfortunate majority (which are mostly middle to low income), debt has become nothing more than a heavy burden; this burden leads to unsolicited phone calls, anger towards our love ones and can also cause low self-esteem.

The stress level connected to debt can cause long term health issues such as constant headaches, back pain, sleepless nights (insomnia) and heartburn. Stress weakens the immune system, which can lead to other unhealthy conditions such as heart disease, strokes or diabetes. Those laden with debt can also become a health risk on their job. Their attention span will become distracted making them more prone to injuries.

The overwhelming thought of debt and not having the ability to pay the debt back has led many to divorce, abuse and in some cases murder/suicide. Many consumers bring this stress on themselves because they lack patience and refuse to take no for an answer. I believe some borrowers have always been confused when it comes to credit worthiness, trying to keep up with the Joneses. This confusion has them "Bound by the debt demon."

"Seek ye first the kingdom of God, and his righteousness; and all these things shall be added unto you."

-Matthew 6:33

Ask Yourself

Before we start let me ask you some questions.

1. Is the vehicle you drive the one you can afford, or the one you wanted?
2. Do you live in the house of your dreams, or the one within your means?
3. Do you need that big screen television?
4. Do you really need those shoes or that piece of jewelry?
5. Are you comfortable in your current financial situation?
6. Have you been able to take a great vacation?
7. Do you spend quality time with your family?
8. Can you leave your children an inheritance according to Proverbs 13:22?

> **NEED**---*verb* **1** required (something) because it is essential or very important.
>
> ---Oxford University Press

You may be wondering what these questions have to do with debt. The answer would be everything. The first four questions deal with material things that are not that important. The last four are very important, or at least should be, because they deal with you the person, your family and stability. Society has shown us that material wealth is a show of status, with little or no focus on the family or the future.

Even though you may want the best for your family, are you giving them the very best that you have to offer? One should never let the wealth of the world dictate how they should live. We all have a certain lifestyle that we should live in, utilizing our current income not our credit. Living with a tremendous amount of debt just to show off, is just not smart.

The Bible tells us that we can have the desires of our heart, whether they are material or spiritual, if we follow Matthew 6:33, which is to Seek first the kingdom of God, and his righteousness; then and only then will those things be added. Many would be surprised at the many blessings that can come their way if they follow these simple words.

Patience is the key, in a world were you can have just about anything by simply pushing a button, many have decided that they no longer have to wait for anything. Many times one may find that if they wait something better will come along. Maybe an unexplained financial gift that comes just in time or maybe a dream home that they desired but never knew they could afford. The Bible tells us in Proverbs that patience is a virtue and should be treasured.

God made a promise to the people of Egypt; He promised them "a land flowing with milk and honey." Many of the people grew impatient and tried to come up with a plan of their own and as a result they were left to wander in the wilderness for 40 years. This type of thinking is why so many are plagued with an enormous amount of debt. God made the promise; we just have to be patient. I am pretty sure that your blessing will not take as long as the people of Egypt, but if it does, I guarantee that it will be worth the wait.

"For there is no respect of persons with God."
-Romans 2:11

The Way I See It

Today is a wonderful day. The temperature is about 80 degrees, the sun is shining and the humidity is just about right. To top it all off I have one of my wife's relatives in from out of town that I have talked to over the phone for many years, but never had a chance to meet. As I sit here on this beautiful Saturday, I began to think of all the things we could be doing, or wondering what type of family plans we could make. Maybe we could just spend the day with friends or hop in the car to take a ride around town, but because of my financial obligations, I am unable to do these things this weekend. Why? Because here I am working the afternoon shift, sitting in front of my computer screen and watching the day roll away. I feel that this is the story of my life. I know I am not alone in this, but I refuse to stay in this situation any longer.

Recently, I began to really look at my financial situation and became extremely frustrated. I realized that I was once again strapped with an over abundance of debt. I never really felt this way before, until my situation became ugly.

My debt overload had begun to put a lot stress on my life and on my family. I had to do something, but in the midst of my helping myself I found that I was also helping others. I realized that I was not alone in this; so I decided to write down some things as they pertain to debt and the problems with it.

The information that I want to share should be life changing, *if* you consider my words. I believe I have been led to write on the problems concerning debt, based on the many problems I have seen and experienced over the years. I believe that a complete understanding for dealing with the problems surrounding debt needs to be discussed, mainly because debt is literally killing people.

For far too long people have let debt destroy their lives. Society has constantly bombarded us with teachings on how to manage, budget or consolidate debt; they never tell you to live without debt. I imagine it would be a very bad business practice to tell people about the problems with debt or why we should hate it and live without it. Debt is a tool designed to keep you in bondage, the Bible tells us in Proverbs 22:7, *"The rich ruleth over the poor, and the borrower is servant to the lender."* You should never fall in love with debt or embrace it in any way.

Bishop Alvernis L. Johnson wrote something in his book called <u>Faith vs. Fantasy</u> that I just had to share. It was a hard word, but right to the point and complemented the thoughts that I wanted to convey in this book. He said, "If some of us admit it, we bought cars on credit that we didn't pay for. We overdrew our accounts. We're the ones who wrote the check that bounced, so when we get the little thin envelope from the bank, let's not go somewhere and get all depressed. We wrote the check when we didn't have the money. That is what fantasy does. It makes you believe you can do anything you want to, live any kind of way you want to live, make all these crazy decisions in life and still think everything is going to work out fine. Reality says you reap what you sow, so right now you have a set of circumstances you don't like. Well guess what? That's the seed you put out. You can't be somewhere with your lips poked out saying: "I don't know why this is happening to me." The Bible says all I have to do is speak it and believe it (1 John 5:15). The Bible also tells us that a wise man, before he builds a house, he sits down and counts up the cost (Luke 14:28)" (Johnson, 2006).

Debt is sold as a golden parachute or a great stabilizer; but in the end you become strapped to it, you depend on it and you learn to live with it. I want to share some practical and Biblical principles that I have learned, and I pray that it can help you in achieving an abundant life free from the dependency on debt. Wouldn't it be great to have a life free from the grips of debt and uncertainty? God wants us to experience an abundant life, a prosperous life as it is written in 3 John v.2, *"Beloved, I wish above all things that thou mayest prosper and be in health, even as thy soul prospereth."*

I wish I could tell you that this is the next great book that will revolutionize your thinking as it pertains to sowing and reaping, or that there are ten simple steps that will make you an instant millionaire. I can say that if you can heed my words and learn to live without debt, you can make great strides in becoming very wealthy. Most people tend to avoid this type of book until they are almost forced to find a solution for their circumstances. I gave one of my classmates the opportunity to read some of the things that I was writing for this book. After a brief glance at the paper, my classmate quickly put it down and said, "I can't read this. I have too much debt, and I try to ignore it." This is the typical response from people who have debt; they try to ignore it as if one day it will go away.

I had always made the assumption that establishing good credit and taking on an abundance of debt would make me an equal, or in other words, I was lead to believe that I would be accepted by society's standards. I eventually found this to be completely untrue. What I found to be true is that God is no respecter of persons, what He does for one He will also do for the other. In knowing this, we can rest on God's Word knowing that we are equal. Debt no longer has to be a burden or take you away from what you should be doing or from what you want to do. God wants us to have an abundant life, and being laced with an over abundance of debt is not the way to accomplish it.

I am sure many of you have had situations in your life where you wanted to help someone but you could not because you were strapped for cash yourself. Maybe you wanted to take a trip or go on a family vacation, but because of your financial obligations to your creditors this became virtually impossible. I have had too many situations in my life where because of my debt load; I have had to say no. This is not a good feeling, especially if you enjoy helping others, or you enjoy spending quality time with your family.

Creditors want you to feel that with an abundance of credit (debt) you can do almost anything, and many of us try to do everything, even though we do not have the finances to back it up. Once you realize that you are in trouble, it is too late, and this is the beginning of one's sorrows. I know what I am talking about; I have been there. I jumped into the debt game early in life. I did not have any knowledge on how maintaining a _reasonable_ credit life really worked.

The Bible tells us in Hosea 4:*6, "My people are destroyed for lack of knowledge."* I was unprepared for what was ahead of me; I was under the impression that banking and loan institutions simply gave you money to do whatever you wanted, and you could take your time paying for it. The trick was that this was exactly what they wanted me to think.

Creditors issue you credit cards from major banking institutions; they send you credit cards from most of the major chain stores (at less than desirable interest rates). They treat you with the utmost respect upon opening these accounts, until it is time to pay them back and you cannot afford to or it becomes a major inconvenience. You then realize that all of the respect that the creditors had for you when you applied for your credit has been thrown out the window. You come face-to-face with the reality of being a high-risk deadbeat with little or no respect from the calling collector. Even though you have a legitimate excuse or a great explanation, you are still considered a high-risk deadbeat.

Ever since I was a teenager, debt has been part of my life; I am not sure if this is normal, but one thing I do know is that I have always loved *things* and try to justify purchasing them. I enjoy splurging on *things* that I felt I deserved because I have worked hard; but once the bill comes, I try my best to desperately pay off the debt as fast as humanly possible. One of the worst feelings is having debt lingering over your head, and for this express reason I have an extreme hatred towards the thought of being bound for life in a sea of debt. The Bible says to owe no man anything, but to love one another. (Romans 13:8) This is the type of debt I can live with.

> *"For ye have need of patience, that, after ye have done the will of God, ye might receive the promise."*
>
> *-Hebrews 10:36*

Joy No More

As a young man growing up in the Motor City (Detroit, MI), my biggest wish was to own a fine automobile. I got my first job, saved my money and purchased my first car for $2500. The pleasure of owning a vehicle free and clear was one of great joy. Most of us start out this way, but as we get older, our desires change, as well as our finances.

For some obvious reasons we seem to always gravitate to a more expensive vehicle than the one we can afford by simply paying cash. When I first set out to buy a vehicle using credit, I was very impatient. I begged my dad to cosign for me, but my dad being a man of great wisdom (and eight children) explained to me the idea of saving my money. Obviously, as a young man, I thought this was foolish conversation. I explained and pleaded my case to my dad until he eventually gave in. I purchased the vehicle, but when it was time to bring the vehicle home, I did not even have enough money to put gas in the car! I had to ask my dad for gas money. This whole car buying experience got worse as time went on. In an effort to maintain and repair the car I had two options, ask my dad for more money or apply for a credit card at the local repair shop; I chose the latter.

Without having any knowledge of how a credit card really worked or how much I was going to have to pay back every month, I quickly abused this card. Instead of using it for the things I needed, I purchased a lot of unnecessary items that I did not need. This process continued until the very affordable payment became very unaffordable. The only thing that I was able to accomplish throughout this whole ordeal was a credit rating, which was just what the creditors wanted me to do so I could be ready for the *next big car purchase*.

As you can see, one of the major pitfalls with credit is neglecting the ability to have patience. Hebrews 10:36 states, *"For ye have need of patience, that, after ye have done the will of God, ye might receive the promise."* In this case, if I would have been patient and saved my money, the things I desired I could have purchased for cash and I would have been much further ahead.

After opening the credit card from the repair facility, I began to get offers from other credit card companies offering me more money to spend! If only I had listened to my dad. I was headed in the wrong direction and it did not take long before reality stepped in. I was in over my head, and I was bound by debt. I was not sure at first what I was feeling, but I knew I did not like it. My carefree life of owning something with no debt had changed for what would seem like an eternity.

Taking my credit card to its limit and owning a vehicle I could barely afford changed my life and my social status. I was the envy of all my friends and family. Everyone assumed I was doing great. I had settled into what seemed like a normal way of living. After keeping up with the payments for a couple of years, I was ready for the *next big car purchase*. I thought for this vehicle that I would be better prepared, but unfortunately I was not.

In an effort to maintain my social status, I once again extended myself and purchased a vehicle that I could not easily afford. One would think that I should have learned my lesson but I did not. I once again used my credit cards to purchase more unnecessary, non-essential items for the vehicle.

This overextension on my credit had me using three paychecks to try and cover my expenses until things got out of control. I was forced to borrow money from my girlfriend and my friends; I even tried (before I became a Christian) to hustle the insurance company (the car was stolen more times than you can imagine). God was trying to tell me something way back then, but I would not listen. You would think that through all of this that I would have received the message, learning from my mistakes and misfortunes. I knew that this car was too much for me, but pride and social acceptance would not allow me to let it go.

I eventually lost the car to repossession and all of the credit I had built up was ruined. I had to learn how to deal in cash once again. I felt betrayed; I felt as if I were an outcast. I was mad at the world for letting this happen to me.

My friends that envied me so while I was driving this expensive vehicle, did not have much to say to me while I was walking. Instead of learning how to live within my means or gaining wisdom from my mistakes, I could not wait to reestablish my credit and start the entire process all over again.

Apparently I learned nothing from this experience. John tells us that, *"The Comforter, which is the Holy Ghost, whom the Father will send in my name, he shall teach you all things, and bring all things to your remembrance…" (John 14:26).* The only thing that I could seem to remember was Proverbs 1:7 which says *"The fear of the Lord is the beginning of knowledge: but fools despise wisdom and instruction."*

> *"Now faith is the substance of things hoped for, the evidence of things not seen."*
>
> *- Hebrews 11:1*

You Are Not Alone

Growing up in a mixed middle-class neighborhood, I assumed everyone's situation was the same concerning debt, until I became older and was able to see some things differently. I noticed that low-income individuals did not have the knowledge or the understanding that would allow them the opportunity to conduct business the same way as their middle-class counterparts; I noticed that their treatment was simply not the same.

When low-income borrowers sit down at a lender's table, they come in looking at different conditions concerning the loan contract, whether it is a higher interest rate or a larger down payment. Because of their low income, they seem to be at-risk before they even take on the loan. This may be a true fact seeing that a large percentage, more than 55% of low income/high risk individuals default or overextend themselves when it comes to credit and/or debt (Live Smart and Prosper.com 2007).

I am not sure if this comes from lack of education concerning debt or if it is just the nature of the beast; I know this is not true for everyone in this percentile, but the numbers are staggering. One thing that I know for sure is that I want to see a change; I want to see people take control of their lives and finances.

Have you ever had your dreams crushed because you were bound by debt? Maybe you wanted to move into a new career that paid less than your current job, but it was always something you wanted to do—something you would enjoy doing.

Maybe you had a desire to move into a new home or start a business, but debt kept you from it. Many entrepreneurs say you need at least 15-35% of your projected budget in order to keep your business afloat for the first year; they also encourage you to keep your debt load as low as possible (most never do).

I had always dreamed of becoming a successful musician playing all around the world. I had all the right equipment, I practiced diligently; I was ready for someone to say "I want to sign you to a contract." As much as I wanted this, I had to put my dreams on hold. I was already established with a home, cars and a young family.

I had a good job working as an electrician and made great money, but I also had debt, which made it hard for me to leave my job and pursue my dream. I was scared and unwilling to take that risk, but I met someone who did. I had a conversation with a young man who is a very prominent Christian musician, who began his career as an electrician. He explained to me that even though he had a great job, he wanted to follow his dream. When he started explaining his story to me and telling me how he and his wife decided that he should follow his dream and move out on faith, I wanted to cry. I was actually a little jealous, but I knew the difference between us. He had a plan and did not drown himself in a world of debt making his dream more obtainable.

We all face some type of life decisions and try to prepare ourselves for them, but somehow debt keeps getting in the way of our plans, as well as the plan that God has put in place for us. Jeremiah 29:11 says, *"For I know the thoughts that I think toward you, saith the Lord, thoughts of peace, and not of evil, to give you an expected end."* Some of those plans include purchasing a home, a luxury vehicle, maybe sending your children to college or maybe even starting a ministry or outreach. For a fortunate few, obtaining and acquiring these things will not become a problem; they will enjoy a prosperous, carefree life, free from the burden of heavy debt. For many others trying to achieve these same goals, life may not be so easy.

Some people will let debt get the best of them. They will let debt ruin their marriages, friendships and job relations. Please understand; debt has its place. It can be a wonderful tool if used correctly, but can become a nightmare if it is abused. Tragedy surrounding debt-related issues has become all too common. Someone takes a life or kills their whole family because the burden of debt has become too much for them; I know it sounds crazy but it happens; I have seen it. There was a time when a female co-worker used her lunch break to rob a bank, even though her job paid decent money. I am not sure what all of the circumstances were surrounding this person, but I am sure she had more money going out than she had coming in. Apparently she thought robbing a bank would help her support her lifestyle. 1Timothy 6:10a says, *"For the love of money is the root of all evil."* Yes, evil!

Why we constantly live above our means and allow debt to wreak havoc on our lives, instead of waiting and being patient, is a mystery that may never be revealed.

"Pride goeth before destruction…"

-Proverbs 16:18a

Misery Loves Company

I had a young man who had just turned 23 years old come to me after his father suddenly passed away; he was scared and nervous to say the least. His father had some possessions but did not have a plan, nor did he leave this young man with any instructions on how to handle them. He left him two very nice vehicles, one was a newer large body vehicle that his dad owned and was paid for. The other was a sporty SUV that was leased.

This young man was in school at the time of his father's death, so he was currently unemployed; this made the situation even harder to deal with. I explained to him that he should first get rid of the leased vehicle.

The plan was to advertise the SUV asking for someone (who could afford it) to take over the payments; this would leave him with the large body vehicle that was paid for. Once the leased vehicle was gone, he could either drive the large body vehicle or sell it and get something a little more practical and pay cash. The young man did not like the idea of driving the large body car, he explained to me that the large body car would not fit his image; he wanted to keep the SUV.

I continually tried to convince him that what people thought of him should not matter; I wanted him to know that the important thing was to get a handle on his current situation. The young man made the decision to keep the SUV and maintain his image. The SUV was eventually repossessed by the bank, and he was forced to sell the large body vehicle to help pay for some other expenses he had acquired. In the end, he was forced to walk. I still talk to the young man, and yes he is still trying to get things in order, but he has told me on many occasions that he respected my suggestions and learned a hard lesson trying to please others instead of doing what was best for him. He has even taken it upon himself to introduce the first edition of this book to others, asking them to read it before they make the same mistakes he made.

Another young entrepreneur that I was introduced to wanted to live the good life. He was pursuing this lifestyle to the point of obsession. This young man owned a very successful business and spent most of his time in business relationships with some very affluent clients. Instead of living within his means, he attempted to mirror his life like those of the people he was working for. This was based on what he had seen in some of his clients' mansion-like estates.

He made the decision to enlarge his own home. He did not have the cash available, so he decided to finance the project with a large bank loan. Things did not go very well for him. Due to this large investment as well as some other obligations, his relationship with his wife was becoming very stressful. Some of the added stress may have been attributed to the fact that his wife, a full-time student and unemployed, was unable to help support the bills that they were acquiring.

When I last talked to this gentleman, he explained to me that he was unable to finish the addition, he and his wife were looking at a possible separation and his home was in foreclosure. The affluent friends he had met over the years were unable to assist him and his family was in no shape to help either.

All is not lost, not every story has a bad ending and some are actually encouraging. This story is based on a conversation that I had with a friend of mine that I will call

Mister. I will not bother telling you who he is; I just wanted to share his story, hoping that you will be encouraged.

Mister graduated from high school and decided to support his country in the United States military. During his time in the military, he was disciplined in the way of becoming a responsible man and a productive U.S. citizen. He was able to achieve this goal, exiting the military with honors. He later met a lovely young lady and married her. Mister and his wife took on good jobs and made plans for a long future with each other and also for their future children.

The couple did everything correctly, but something happened. With their financial situation seeming to be in order, Mister's wife decided she should stay home and raise their children. On the surface, this seemed to be a great idea because they planned for the future.

Being a responsible father and husband, Mister decided to purchase a larger home for his family in a quiet suburb; he also purchased a larger car. Basically he did everything one would do to provide a better life for his or her family.

Mister knew this was a stretch, but he figured they could make it work, but it did not. They were on the verge of losing the home they had so proudly purchased.

Although it hurt his pride to ask, he looked to his family for help. To their surprise the house was saved; this scenario played out a few more times until all of their resources were exhausted.

Debt had overwhelmed Mister, threatening him the repossession of their home and vehicles, with no other hope in sight and with what would seem like a loss of their integrity. The credit companies now treated a man, who had fought for his country, raised a loving family and did everything correctly, like a second-class citizen.

For several years those who had helped him in the past ridiculed Mister. With no other options, he was forced to live with family members.

This entire situation taught Mister a valuable lesson (even if it was a hard one). Mister and his wife educated themselves and vowed to never let debt rule them again. They have also taken the necessary steps to help other willing individuals free themselves from debt.

These are just a few of the real life situations that many face everyday and I am sure that you could add some stories of your own. The most important thing to remember is to be comfortable with who you are and where you are.

"...Fools despise wisdom and instruction."
-Proverbs 1:7b

More Bad News

People allow themselves to get in trouble by taking on debt for someone else by becoming a co-signer, or in other words a guarantee to pay for someone else. The book of wisdom that is Proverbs talks to us very clearly about becoming a co-signer. Proverbs 22:26,27 says, *"Do not co-sign another person's note or put up a guarantee for someone else's loan. If you can't pay it, even your bed will be snatched from under you." (NLT)*

That Scripture sounds pretty clear to me, but let us look further at what God says about becoming a co-signer. Proverbs 11:15 states: *"Guaranteeing a loan for a stranger is dangerous; it is better to refuse than to suffer later"(NLT)*. What about Proverbs 6:1-5 that says: *"My child, if you co-sign a loan for a friend or guarantee the debt of someone you hardly know – if you have trapped yourself by your agreement and are caught by what you said-follow my advice and save yourself, for you have placed yourself at your friend's mercy. Now swallow your pride; go and beg to have your name erased. Don't put it off; do it now! Don't rest until you do. Save yourself like a gazelle escaping from a hunter, like a bird fleeing from a net" (NLT).*

I do not want to discourage you from helping someone get ahead in life, just remain wise about it. Do you really want to be a guarantee for someone else? There are plenty of other ways a person can get a decent start without having to use someone else's name to achieve it.

In an article written by the Bankrate.com (2006), a girlfriend wanted to know if she should cover her boyfriend's debt totaling more than $30,000. The young lady wrote in for some sound financial advice, but the counselor assigned to her case was apparently a father and was very concerned for her. He said, "As a father my advice would be to run away from this guy as far and as quickly as possible." The young lady was worried that her boyfriend would leave her if she said no, but the advice the counselor gave her was firm.

The boyfriend apparently had little respect for his girlfriend, seeing that he wanted her to help him cancel $30,000 of his personal debt, for the second time, within three years of each other. The Counselor was very upset that the young lady would even consider this situation, stating that the boyfriend was either "oblivious or ignorant" about how to manage his finances. He went on to say, "You, however, apparently understand the financial score and realize that by helping pay down his debt, you would be encouraging him to do it yet again, but this time with your money! If, for some unexplained reason, you don't want to take my fatherly advice and dump the boyfriend, there are several things you might get him to try that may help him while not hurting you financially in the process."

As you can see from this story, debt is about to ruin a relationship. Many couples that are facing some type of financial trouble in their relationships may not agree with each other's money management skills, but seem to find a common ground, which is divorce. Relationships seem to play an important role when one deals with debt. When you are in a relationship with someone, there is a certain amount of trust that both parties have for each other. When the trust factor fails due to bad money management decisions, couples begin to argue. A spouse will argue with another spouse to the point where verbal abuse, violence, even assault will take over the relationship, leading the couple to eventually divorce.

I have noticed that in various communities foreclosure is also on the rise. I personally know of several families that have been removed from their home due to a foreclosure. These people all had jobs and stability, and they were able to maintain a middle-class lifestyle, but somehow they let debt get the best of them. I am pretty sure they did not plan for things to work out the way they did, but this type of thing happens all of the time.

Maybe it's because some middle-class Americans were dealt a bad blow from the start. Most middle-class Americans have never received an inheritance, nor had a windfall of wealth come their way that could help them in achieving a good jumpstart in life.

Most people are taught to live the simple life. They are told to get a good job, establish and maintain some type of credit, buy a home in a decent neighborhood and drive an affordable vehicle. This type of teaching is very practical, and helps people to feel comfortable. It also gives them a sense of success. Somewhere down the line, we have lost this teaching and have decided to go the road that society wants us to travel. This strong influence that permeates the middle-class community is the distorted mentality that you should keep up with "the Joneses."

You know the Joneses: their grass always *looks* greener, their vehicles *look* more expensive, their houses *seem* larger and they *look* happier. It could be a matter of perception, but depending on their life choices, it could be real. Champions make decisions that create the future they desire, while losers make decisions that create the present they desire.

> **LOOK**---*verbs 1 have* the appearance or give the impression of being.
>
> ---Oxford University Press

Perception tarnishes the view of what it means to live a simple life. Assuming the Joneses success, wealth and happiness is real, it would be attributable to their life choices and their means. As long as they made the right choices and are living within their means, life for the Joneses is simple, for others, chaos and confusion will become the order of the day, and God is not the author of confusion.

"A fool and his money are soon parted."

-Thomas Tusser

Important Facts and Statistics

USA Today published an article entitled "High Earners Can Still Struggle" that I found to be amazing. The article had some staggering statistics based on the debt load that high money earners have and are unable to or struggle to pay back. The article was very lengthy and thorough dealing with everything from credit cards, personal loans, mortgages, school loans and tuition.

I focused on some key elements of the article, in which some of the information was based on surveys conducted by independent agencies. Assuming the people who were surveyed told the unadulterated truth, these statistics are very scary. Although I was not as shocked as I should have been, I was amazed because I, like most people, believed the grass was greener, or should I say life was better on the other side. After reading this article I was somewhat excited because I knew the God had put me on track with my study and with my writings.

One of the statistics that caught my attention almost immediately was discovering that nearly one in five workers (19%) who earn $100,000 or more report that they often or always live paycheck to paycheck, although 18% save $1,000 or more per month and 30% save $250 or less. (USA Today 2007)

Some other statistics in this article state that:

- 12% save $100 or less per month.

- 7% don't have monthly savings.

- 10% of those who make over $100,000 don't participate in a 401(k), IRA or retirement program.

- 18% of employees earning $100,000 could continue their lifestyle for one month or less if they lost their income. Twelve percent of these high earners say they have no money left over after paying debts.

- The surges in housing costs have led employees to devote a larger percentage of their income toward their mortgages. From 2004 to 2005, median incomes rose just 1.1% to $46,326.

- In just one year the number of households with housing cost burdens greater than 30% of their income climbed by 2.3 million, hitting a record 37.3 million in 2005.

- Adjustable-rate mortgages grew from 13% for a growing number of homeowners in mid-2003 to 35% in mid-2005.

Many high wage earners who live paycheck to paycheck are simply overspending and using credit cards or other debt sources to sustain their lifestyle. High-income households, on average, spend more of their income on food away from home, entertainment, clothing and services, according to data from the Bureau of Labor Statistics.

There is an additional sign of social unacceptability attached to those who earn middle-to-high incomes (Those who have chosen to live without savings, or have accumulated a huge amount of debt). Many of those in this income bracket believe that they should be able to handle their finances and fear the disapproval of others who may view them as reckless spenders. According to the USA Today article, many credit advisers see this as an ongoing problem in the middle-to-high income brackets.

Credit allows people and organizations to do things that they otherwise would not be able to do. Commonly, people use credit to purchase houses, cars and many other things too expensive to buy with cash on hand. Companies also use debt in many ways to leverage the investment made in their private equity. This leverage, the proportion of debt to equity, is considered important in determining the riskiness of an investment; the more debt per equity, the riskier.

Islam forbids lending with interest just as the Catholic church did long ago. The Jewish teaching of the Torah Hebrew Bible states that all debts should be erased every seven years and again every 50 years. An overload of debt from a religious viewpoint is frowned upon because of the adverse effect it can have on an individual. The stress and worry that is associated with debt are all considred unhealthy to one's Christian lifestyle, and are even considered to be sins.

Despite a growing economy, a rising stock market and stronger corporate earnings that are helping many to get rich, many middle-class Americans are caught in an unprecedented squeeze that makes them increasingly unstable.

Families are continuing to live beyond their means, finding it very difficult just to pay for the basics. Middle-class families are slowly sinking into a life of poverty. They are not only spending their current income but they are also spending their future income having to pay back all of the money they have borrowed. Some may find themselves in this situation due to the mistakes they have made financially. For others it is a way of life that they have learned to live with. Regardless of which side of the fence they are on, it is still a large problem.

Many middle-class Americans seems to be less prepared for an economic emergency, such as losing a job or visiting an emergency room. America has not seen these types of problems since the late 1970's.

Health care and health insurance costs are soaring. We have 47 million uninsured individuals in America. Health care costs tend to take a big chunk out of the budgets of many who do have coverage. Two out of five adults (43%) who buy individual polices, and one in four whose employers help pay for their coverage, spend more than

10% of their incomes on premiums and out-of-pocket medical expenses according to the Commonwealth Fund.

Many years ago settlers came over from foreign countries and worked on farms or in shipyards. They helped build a country that they were not even born in, hoping to one-day become a citizen. Things were much simpler then. Immigrants did not care about what society was doing; they just wanted an opportunity. Somehow we have forgotten this simple way of life; instead we spend our time playing catch-up to people who can afford to live a grander lifestyle.

We seemed to be plagued with a false ideal of what it really means to have a good life. You see it everyday—on your television, in the newspaper or in a magazine. America is obsessed with the lifestyles of the rich and famous. We want to know where they live, what they are driving and where they go. The list just goes on and on. Did you ever think you would see the day when a t-shirt would sell for $200 just because a famous celebrity was seen wearing it?

Statistically the average American carries eight credit cards with an average household balance of $9000. Those numbers are even worse once a mortgage is added.

According to the Federal Reserve, the total U.S. household mortgage debt now exceeds $8 trillion. Americans have taken debt to a whole new level! Inflated expectations about what constitutes an American middle-class life leads many people into the kind of spending decisions that endanger their long-term financial security. These individuals are those who are unable to wait, who refuse to save money in order to pay for the things they want. They also lack patience. These individuals are the ones who wind up with insurmountable credit card debt and who overspend on homes or other extravagant amenities.

In an effort to obtain some of these extravagancies we look to our lending intuitions for a loan. With a reasonable credit rating, the institution will usually extend to you some type of credit. The process is so easy; I can see why people get carried away. The feeling of a new purchase will have you singing praises until it is time to pay it back, and then those horrid monthly payments begin.

Unfortunately, for some the loan will become delinquent. Debtors will try to come up with clever ways to get themselves out of debt; this only makes matters worse. Or you begin to borrow from friends and family in order to pay the loan off early, but this only increases our financial obligation. This scenario has become all too familiar.

Lenders simply do not care who can afford to borrow; they are in this business to make money. Prior to the advent of the credit scoring system, lenders were much more conservative. Today, lenders are using some very clever marketing techniques that cater to those with a higher credit rating.

Take some time to read the small print that is advertised in many lenders low-interest rate promotions. You will find that in certain parts of the country credit card lenders can charge up to 30 % or more just in interest. You also have to be careful because many lenders also include many fees and charges that are only explained in the small print.

To maintain day-to-day consumption and current lifestyles many Americans are taking on record amounts of consumer debt (approximately $5.2 trillion since 2001). In June 2006, it was reported that families took on debt equivalent to 129% of their disposable incomes, which was a big increase from the 96% reported in March 2001.

Many homeowners are tapping into the equity in their homes, assuming more debt to pay for the various expenditures they have incurred. Regretfully falling home prices could force many of these middle-class families into foreclosure or back into apartments losing all of the equity they have accumulated over the years.

With the exception of a few entrepreneurs and self-made business owners, there are fewer good jobs for those who don't have college educations. Education was, and still is, a positive ticket to a more affluent life. Although there are no guarantees that a degree will earn you big bucks, it definitely helps to hold one. Eight million vets grabbed this ticket in the wake of World War II, which helped fuel a huge expansion in America's middle-class.

A decline in manufacturing and increased globalization makes it tougher than ever to get into the middle-class without a college education. Globalization and outsourcing are snipping away at blue-collar and white-collar jobs as well. A fast-evolving economy means few can be content to end their educations after four years.

The cost of a college education has skyrocketed and financial aid has not kept up; loans have replaced grants as the primary source of financial aid and too many students graduate with crippling debt.

Middle-class families are also struggling with the ballooning costs of higher education. The total cost of tuition, fees and room and board at four-year public colleges has increased 44% in the past four years.

Maybe you are thinking you can avoid all of this by becoming your own boss; think again! Most new businesses are small and self-financed. The typical cost to start a business is about $10,000. The founders of these businesses will usually borrow from any available source be it friends, family, personal loans or credit cards. They will borrow up to $18,000 per year (Money 2007). P.61

The bottom line here is that debt does not discriminate. Until we stop living beyond our means, we will continue to go deeper into debt.

"Wisdom is the principal thing; therefore get wisdom: and with all thy getting get understanding."

-Proverbs 4:7

Sub-Primed

According to the Center for Responsible Lending (2007), an astonishing 2.2 million sub-prime home loans (which are high cost loans given to individuals with a blemished credit record) made in recent years have already failed or will end in foreclosure. These foreclosures could cost as much as $164 billion—an amount that could send more than four million children through college.

One in five families who get a sub-prime mortgage today will lose their home to foreclosure. For most people, owning a home is their best chance to achieve sustainable economic security. Losing that home, in many cases, means losing life savings.

This epidemic of foreclosures will have a negative impact on the economy as a whole, with potentially devastating consequences for African-American and Latino communities, who receive the highest share of sub-prime loans.

The system may be against many of these borrowers. Examining 50,000 sub-prime loans, the Center's researchers found these groups were almost a third more likely to get a high-priced loan than white American borrowers with the same credit profile. The findings show that a decade of work by the civil rights movement to bring fairness and opportunity to all homebuyers is still unfinished.

The sub-prime loan started out as a great idea but failed many. Future homeowners with sub par credit were given loans at a lower interest rate that would increase over the course of a few years. This type of loan is similar to an adjustable rate loan, but instead of starting with a very low interest rate (four or five percent) many loans started in the eight to nine percent range and went up from there making the loan very unaffordable, and forcing many into foreclosure.

Many people who were either living on the edge or had not taken the necessary steps to build an adequate credit profile suffered. Instead of enjoying the home that they longed for, they found themselves deeper and deeper in debt as the interest rates of their loans continued to climb along with their payments. The end result is that many have lost the place they once called home.

This situation has turned into one of the worst economic threats since the 1930's, when the Great Depression riddled its way through most of America. With nearly 2 million homes facing foreclosure in the next two or three years, it is no wonder why the government had to step in and help curtail these reckless lending practices. The Federal Reserve has issued what they are calling a Wall Street bailout, which will create a dozen new rules for the lending institutions.

Many sub-primed Americans are paying a heavy price for the lending institutions quest for greed, but it is not the end of the world. Time does indeed heal all things, and with that time those who were affected by the sub-prime fiasco can take the necessary steps to be better prepared for their real home.

"...I have set before you life, and death, blessing and cursing: therefore choose life that both thou and thy seed may live."

-Deuteronomy 30:19

Help Is Here

The credit privilege needs to be fully understood, and it has to be respected as well. Many people, who have been in serious financial trouble, have freed themselves from the grips of debt. The key point is to get educated; to learn as much as you can just as you would with any other subject that you are interested in.

It is easy to know if you are in trouble. You have to think and ask yourself, are your debts causing you any level of discomfort? If they are, it is almost certain that you are having a problem with debt. Here are just a few suggestions that have helped others:

- Avoid telemarketing "debt counselors" since many of these companies charge outrageous fees and have been known to be great con artists. They only come to take what little you have left, knowing that you are in a desperate situation.

- Target bills and zap them one by one. I would suggest finding a method that would work best for you, a method such as the traditional debt-snowball method of paying off the smallest debt first while making minimum payments on the rest. Then as you finish paying off the smallest debt, add the old payment to the new smallest debt. And so on.

- Remain cautious and avoid the temptation of sliding back into debt. Yes, things will come up and you will deem it necessary to use those credit cards, but you must stay the course. Remember that patience is the key.

Once you have changed the way you approach debt know that there is a plan, and it is deceptively simple:

- **Spend less than you make**. The key to making any financial progress is to live within your means. Think it is impossible on your income? You are almost certainly wrong. And in the end, you really do not have a choice.

- **Limit your debt**. It is costing you unnecessary interest and leaves you vulnerable to the slightest economic setback. The more you owe, the fewer choices you have.

- **Save for a rainy day.** Even $500 in the bank could allow you to weather day-to-day crisis like a car repair that could otherwise push you over the edge.

- **Plan for retirement.** Start early; avoid borrowing or using your retirement dollars for any reason. Even a small amount, scraped together and invested over a lifetime, offers a much more comfortable retirement.

- **Avoid debt all together.** This may be a bit extreme, but it works.

- **Stay sharp.** You are the captain of your financial ship. You have to look for new opportunities and spot potential dangers.

- **Pray.** This should actually be first on your list. Remember to seek God first, and He *will* supply all of your needs.

Also be sure to investigate some of the great books, websites and service agencies dedicated to helping those who want to learn more about debt management, debt reduction or money management. Many of these resources are both practical and Biblical; choosing any one of these resources can be very beneficial.

I have had and found great success with two online resources:

- Money Central.msn.com

- DFA Central.com

Both of these web sites are packed with a wealth of information pertaining to debt, debt management and money saving strategies.

There are many books available that deal with debt solutions, with strategically paying off debt, or with managing debt. There are two books in general that I can recommend. These books helped revolutionize my thinking when it comes to overall debt strategies. John Avanzini calls one book <u>Debt Reduction Strategies</u>. In Avanzini's book he breaks down practical principals, which if followed correctly will help you reduce your debt and move into a debt-free society. Another great book is by Ric Edelman <u>The Truth about Money</u>, which is a comprehensive, practical, "how-to" manual on financial planning. These two books are great representations of Biblical (Avanzini) and practical (Edelman) applications that are available to you.

Credit counseling and service agencies can also be a valuable asset in your debt reduction plan. These agencies will help you learn how to read and understand your credit report, credit scores and offers you an opportunity (based on certain conditions) to have negative items removed from your credit report. Recently the Internal Revenue Service found that 41 out of 63 credit counseling companies it examined were preying on debtors. So find a counselor certified by the National Foundation for Credit Counseling. These companies can help you negotiate with creditors since debt collectors buy uncollected debt from your creditors for literally pennies on the dollar.

Find a counseling agency you can trust, one that has a positive track record. I would suggest a non-profit or Christian based agency. Non-profit credit counseling agencies offer confidential and professional budget counseling, debt management and financial education programs to consumers across America. God says in Proverbs 16:3 *"Commit thy works unto the LORD, and thy thoughts shall be established."*

"A set back, is a setup for a come back."

-Author unknown

The New Beginning

Many people pick up books like this to find a quick solution to a life-long problem; unfortunately, it is not going to be that easy. Breaking free from debt is like going on a diet, it takes discipline, training, motivation and prayer. It is time to go on a "debt diet." In other words, it is time to purge your system from that "I need it now" syndrome.

Life is what we make out of it so why spend your life stressed out with debt overload. As I have mentioned before, debt is just a tool and nothing more and should be treated as one. Just as you would with any tool in the tool shed, you should only pull it out when you need it. Why pull out the lawn mower when it is snowing?

My original idea was to allow the reader to make his or her own decisions regarding a solution to a problem. I did not want to create the idea that my solution was the only solution, nor did I want to create a sowing and reaping type controversy. I wanted to give the reader a solid foundation to make his or her own decisions, but then I realized the following information was too important to miss.

Biblically speaking I believe it is very important to bind the demon that wants to keep you bound and in debt. Matthew 18:18 says, *"Whatsoever ye shall bind on earth shall be bound in heaven: and whatsoever ye shall loose on earth shall be loosed in heaven."* Remember, God wants you to be the lender not the borrower.

Stay positive and continue to say the right things regarding your situation, Mark 11:23, says to speak with confidence in faith without doubt. We can say to this literal mountain move and it has to move. If you are facing an abundance of debt, speak to it with confidence. Speak God's Word to it, knowing that the Word has power, life and is our refuge.

One of the most important things in your endeavor to free yourself is to have an opened mind and an opened hand. I have struggled with this myself; you have to be willing to not only give, but to also receive. Giving is one of the key principles that God commanded when He said, *"Give and it shall be given" (Luke 6:38).* Try to understand that a closed fist is unable to receive. Ephesians 6:8 says,

"Knowing that whatsoever good thing any man doeth, the same shall he receive of the Lord, whether he be bond or free."

Today can become a day of new beginnings; debt no longer has to be your god. I encourage you to seek God and allow Him to guide you, remaining prayerful, knowing that God has promised His best for you.

The Bible says, *"Ask, and it shall be given you; seek, and ye shall find; knock, and it shall be opened unto you"* (Luke 11:9). Information is available to anyone that is willing to let debt go. Learn to hate debt just as I have. I can assure you that you will do everything in your power to free yourself from it, and learn to live a prosperous life without it.

Remain cautious of the enemy and his attempt to deceive you. The Bible tells us in Deuteronomy 11:16, *"Take heed to yourselves, that your heart be not deceived, and ye turn aside, and serve other gods, and worship them."* Most people fail to realize that debt *is* a god; we are enslaved to it, bound by it and spend countless years hoping to break free from it. But debt still remains one of the worst burdens a person can face.

I pray that you will be motivated to seek financial freedom, free from the burdens of debt and free from a lifestyle of uncertainty and despair. Move forward so that you may see the promise of God concerning you. It is time to become smarter and more cautious than ever before. You have to continue obeying those deceptively simple rules, making smart decisions, feeling comfortable within our means and maintaining the lifestyle for which we are suited.

One thing is certain. Wherever you currently stand on the economic ladder, the surest way to rise is to pull yourself up. Just know that many have overcome the grip of debt. Even though it may seem like you cannot make it or that your situation is hopeless, with persistence and prayer you will begin enjoying a life completely free from debt. Remember this is just one of the many resources available to you, I encourage you to take advantage of the many resources I have listed in the back of the book.

Someone once said to me, "A set back, is a setup for a come back." It is time to stop living in the red; debt does not have to control you. Debt can be a wonderful tool if not abused. Life is simple; let us keep it that way.

"The rich ruleth over the poor, and the borrower is servant to the lender."

-Proverbs 22:7

Sources

Armour, S. (2007, June 28) "High earners can still struggle." USA Today Money. p. B3

Avanzini J. (1990) Debt Reduction Strategies (3rd ed) Hurst, TX: HIS Publishing Co.

Bankrate.com. (2006). http://articles.moneycentral.msn.com/SavingsandDebt/ManageDebt/ManageDebt.aspx

Center for Responsible Lending. (2007). http://www.responsiblelending.org/press/statements/page.jsp?itemID=31217027

Commonwealth fund. (2007). http://www.commonwealthfund.org/surveys/

DFA Central. (2008). www.dfacentral.com

Edelman, R. (2000). "The Truth about Money" (2nd ed) New York, NY: Harper Collins Publisher's Inc.

Federal Reserve. (2007).
http://www.federalreserve.gov/releases/

Johnson, A.L. (2006). <u>Faith vs. Fantasy.</u> Saginaw, MI: City of Light Publishing.

Live Smart and Prosper. (2007)
http://www.lendsmartandprosper.com/index.php

MSN Money Central. (2006).
http://moneycentral.msn.com/home.asp

MSN Money Women in Red. (2006).
http://articles.moneycentral.msn.com/SavingandDebt/ManageDebt/TheWorstKindOfDebtChargingTheGroceries.aspx

Oxford University Press. (2007). http://www.oup.co.uk

Regnier, P. (2007, July) "Getting Rich in America." <u>Money Magazine</u> p.75-77

NOTES

NOTES